W9-AZP-072

The QUICK Cook

To Harriet —
Happy Cooking!
Doris Koplin

GREAT DINNERS PREPARED WITH EASE

DORIS KOPLIN

© 2002 by Doris Koplin. All rights reserved.

All recipes created and developed by Doris Koplin
Cover design and book layout by Jaime Sherman

Web site: www.thequickcook.com
E-mail: thequickcook@mindspring.com

When I'm asked what life is all about,
my one-word answer is always the same:
Family!

This book is dedicated with love to family members
who grace my table at least once a week:

My children, Janis and Marvin Zagoria and Kal and Charlene Koplin;
my grandchildren, Alex Koplin, Amy Koplin, Daniel Zagoria
and Haley Zagoria, and especially my husband, Beryl

Special thanks to:

Heather Dabney, Kirby Frank, Paul Glickstein,
Rick Goldman, Beryl Koplin, Charlene Koplin,
Jim Rice, Nancy Rocquemore, Jaime Sherman,
Margaret Ann Surber, Janis Zagoria and Natalie Zieky

Cook it Fresh!
Cook it Fast!
Cook it Fabulous!

Introduction
THE QUICK COOK

Who wants to cook quickly? Everyone!

Welcome, then, to *The Quick Cook!*

The Quick Cook is a personal collection of fast-fix, easily created dishes — perfect for today's hectic pace. These recipes are not only user-friendly and fun to prepare; they're sensible, health-savvy and fanatic about good taste.

Want to prepare a unique and complete one-dish dinner? Flip to **Dinner in a Dish in a Dash** for a feast of delicious ideas. The suggested components blend well, and can be mixed and matched in many creative ways. When time permits, the **First Course** and **Dessert** sections offer options for expanding and completing a great meal.

The Quick Cook was developed in an effort to encourage the return of the family dinner (remember them?!). It enables today's busy families to prepare and enjoy the all-important evening meal with fun, love and tasty results. It is my hope that these recipes will engage your imagination and provide you with new and quick ideas for dining at home.

Doris Koplin

QUICK TIPS
for the Quick Cook

▶ **PLAN AHEAD**

Organize, organize, organize!

Plan a week's worth of menus at a time

Shop with a list

Shop only once a week, or twice to fill in fresh items

Don't shop when you're hungry

Don't compromise freshness or quality

▶ **GET READY TO COOK**

Read recipes thoroughly before you begin

Have all the necessary equipment (utensils, bowls, etc.) out and ready

Measure all your ingredients before beginning

Always season to taste

Enlist the help of family or friends, and involve the kids!

Clean up as you go

▶ **SERVE WITH STYLE**

Use attractive serving pieces

Serve milk, juice and other drinks from pitchers, not cartons

Garnish whenever possible — we eat first with our eyes!

Fresh flowers on the table add even more to your enjoyment

The First
COURSE

Spreadables, Salads, Soups and More

The First Course

SPREADABLES

SALADS

SOUPS

AND MORE

Sun-Dried
TOMATO
Spread

▸ 1 clove garlic, peeled

1 8-ounce package light cream cheese

3 ounces (1 1/2 cups) sun-dried tomatoes, rehydrated
(cover with boiling water for 2 minutes and drain)

3 tablespoons pesto, prepared or homemade

1/4 cup grated Parmesan cheese

Assorted crackers

Drop garlic into work bowl of food processor fitted with steel blade
and chop. Add cream cheese, tomatoes, pesto and Parmesan.
Process until well combined. Transfer to serving dish and sprinkle
with additional Parmesan if desired. Serve with assorted crackers.

SERVES 10-12

Smoked Trout
SPREAD

▸ 8 ounces smoked trout
1 8-ounce package light cream cheese
Juice of 1/2 lemon
1 teaspoon lemon pepper
Party rye slices

Place trout, cream cheese, lemon juice and lemon pepper in work bowl of a food processor fitted with steel blade. Process until ingredients are well combined. Transfer to a serving dish. Sprinkle lighly with additional lemon pepper. Serve with party rye slices.

SERVES 6-8

VEGGIE
Spread

- 6 green onions, with tops, cut into chunks
  1 red bell pepper, cored, seeded and cut into chunks
  1 8-ounce package light cream cheese, cut into cubes
  Salt and pepper to taste

Place onions and pepper in work bowl of food processor fitted with steel blade. Pulse 3 or 4 times to chop. Add cream cheese, salt and pepper. Process briefly, just until ingredients have combined well. Serve with crackers and crudités.

NOTE: Can be prepared a day or two ahead. Refrigerate until ready to serve.

SERVES 6-8

Carmelized Onions with
GOAT CHEESE
Bruschetta

- 1 tablespoon butter
  1 tablespoon light olive oil
  4 onions, thinly sliced
  2 tablespoons dark brown sugar
  2 tablespoons balsamic vinegar
  1 4-ounce package goat cheese (chèvre)
  Toasted french bread (baguette) slices

Melt butter with oil in a large skillet. Add onions and cook over low heat 20-25 minutes, stirring frequently. Add sugar and vinegar. Mix well and cook 3-4 minutes longer. Remove from heat. Spread toast slices with goat cheese and top with onions. Serve warm.

SERVES 4-6

Black or White BEAN DIP

- 1 clove garlic, minced
- 1 tablespoon granulated sugar
- 1/4 cup chopped fresh basil
- 2 tablespoons chopped fresh parsley
- 1 teaspoon salt
- 1/8 teaspoon freshly ground black pepper
- 1/2 cup red wine vinegar
- 1 cup canola oil
- 1 16-ounce can black or white (cannellini) beans, rinsed and drained

Place garlic, sugar, basil, parsley, salt, pepper and vinegar in work bowl of food processor fitted with steel blade. With machine running, slowly pour the oil through the feed tube. Remove dressing to a bowl.

Place beans in work bowl of food processor. Add 1/2 cup dressing to the beans and process until smooth. Add more dressing if desired.

Serve with crudités: sliced carrots, cucumbers, zucchini, yellow squash, cherry tomatoes, snow peas and/or other raw vegetables of your choice.

SERVES 8-10

Chopped Salad
WITH BASIL VINAIGRETTE

▸ **SALAD**

1 red bell pepper, cored, seeded and cut in 1/2" dice

1 yellow bell pepper, cored, seeded and cut in 1/2" dice

1 cucumber, cut into 1/2" dice

3 green onions, thinly sliced

1 large tomato, seeded and cut into chunks

1 15-ounce can chickpeas, drained

1/2 cup Basil Vinaigrette

Romaine lettuce leaves

▸ **VINAIGRETTE**
(Yield: 1 1/2 cups)

1 clove garlic, peeled

20 fresh basil leaves

1 teaspoon Dijon mustard

1 teaspoon salt

Freshly ground black pepper to taste

1 tablepoon granulated sugar

1/2 cup red wine vinegar

1 cup canola oil

VINAIGRETTE: Drop garlic into work bowl of food processor fitted with steel blade and chop. Add basil, mustard, salt, pepper, sugar and vinegar. With processor running, add oil through feed tube in a slow, steady stream.

SALAD: In a large bowl, combine the peppers, cucumber, green onions, tomatoes and chickpeas. Pour dressing over vegetables, and toss to coat. Chill for 2-3 hours. Serve over a bed of lettuce leaves.

NOTE: Other vegetables of your choice can be used or added, such as diced carrots, green peppers, green or black olives, etc.

SERVES 4

FIELD GREENS
with Lime Dressing

▸ **LIME DRESSING**

1 clove garlic, minced

1 teaspoon salt

A few grinds fresh black pepper

1 teaspoon granulated sugar

Juice of 1 lime

1/4 cup canola oil

▸ **SALAD**

1/2 pound assorted field greens

1/2 cup sliced toasted almonds for garnish

In a small bowl, combine the garlic, salt, pepper, sugar and lime juice. Whisk in the oil in a slow, steady stream until well combined.

Place greens in a bowl, toss lightly with dressing and garnish with toasted almonds.

SERVES 4

Bread & Tomato SALAD

▸ 1 pound 2-day-old country-style bread, crusts removed and cut into 1/2" cubes (about 6 cups)

2 pounds ripe tomatoes, at room temperature, cored, seeded and cut into 1/2" cubes (about 4 cups)

1 cup diced red onion

12 fresh basil leaves, washed, dried and shredded, plus additional sprigs for garnish

1 cup light olive oil

1/2 cup red wine vinegar

Salt and freshly ground black pepper

In a large bowl, toss the bread, tomatoes, onions and shredded basil leaves together until well-mixed. Drizzle the oil and vinegar over the salad and toss to mix thoroughly. Season to taste with salt and pepper and let stand for 10 minutes before serving. Garnish with sprigs of fresh basil.

SERVES 6

Red Cabbage SLAW

▶ 1 small head red cabbage, finely choppped
6 green onions, thinly sliced on an angle
2 carrots, shredded
1 tomato, seeded and diced
4 tablespoons light mayonnaise
4 tablespoons red wine vinegar
1 tablespoon granulated sugar
1 teaspoon salt
1/4 teaspoon pepper

In a large bowl, combine the cabbage, onions, carrots and tomatoes.
In a separate bowl, whisk together the mayonnaise, vinegar, sugar, salt and pepper. Pour dressing over slaw, and mix well. Chill until ready to serve.

SERVES 6

Crudités
WITH REMOULADE SAUCE

▸ **REMOULADE SAUCE**

1 cup light mayonnaise

1/4 cup chopped sour pickle

1 tablespoon chopped capers

1 tablespoon chopped fresh parsley

1 teaspoon anchovy paste

1 teaspoon Dijon mustard

1/2 teaspoon dried tarragon

3/4 cup cocktail sauce or ketchup

▸ **CRUDITÉS**

Whole baby carrots

Cucumber slices

Cherry tomatoes

Sugar snap peas

Strips of red, yellow and orange bell peppers

In a medium bowl, whisk together the mayonnaise, pickle, capers, parsley, anchovy paste, mustard, tarragon and cocktail sauce or ketchup. Store in refrigerator until ready to serve.

Place a small bowl of sauce in the center of a large serving platter. Arrange vegetables around the bowl of sauce for dipping.

SERVES 10-12

MELON & BERRIES
with Ginger Ale

▸ 1 cantaloupe
1 cup raspberries, washed and dried on paper towel
1 cup blackberries, washed and dried on paper towel
2 cups cold ginger ale
Mint sprigs for garnish

Cut cantaloupe in half and remove seeds. With a melon baller, scoop melon into small balls and place in a bowl. Add the berries and toss gently to mix well.

To serve, place fruit in dessert glasses (stemmed or other). Pour cold ginger ale over fruit. Garnish with mint sprigs and serve at once.

SERVES 4-6

Chunky
GAZPACHO

- 2 cloves garlic, minced

  1 teaspoon salt

  1/8 teaspoon teaspoon freshly ground black pepper

  2 tablespoons olive oil

  2 tablespoons vinegar

  4 cups canned tomato purée or 8 large tomatoes, peeled, seeded and puréed

  1 cucumber, peeled, seeded and diced

  2 tomatoes, seeded and diced

  1 red bell pepper, cored, seeded and diced

  3 green onions, thinly sliced

  1 cup croutons

  Chopped parsley for garnish

In a large bowl, combine the garlic, salt, pepper, oil, vinegar and tomato purée. Mix well. Add cucumber, diced tomatoes, pepper and green onions. Stir to mix well. Chill 2-3 hours or until ready to serve.

To serve, ladle soup into 4 serving bowls and serve with croutons. Garnish with chopped parsley.

SERVES 4

Pickled Beet Soup
WITH CUCUMBERS

- 1 16-ounce jar sliced pickled beets, drained (reserve liquid)
  1/2 small onion, cut into chunks
  1/2 teaspoon salt
  1/8 teaspoon freshly ground black pepper
  Juice of 1 lemon
  2 teaspoons granulated sugar
  1/4 cup reserved beet liquid
  1/4 cup sour cream
  1/2 cucumber, seeded and diced

  Additional sour cream for serving
  Chopped chives

Place beets, onions, salt, pepper, lemon juice, sugar and beet liquid in
a blender and process until well combined. Add sour cream and process briefly.
Pour beet soup into a bowl and chill until ready to serve.

To serve, add diced cucumber to soup; mix well. Ladle soup into 4 serving bowls
and top each with a dollop of sour cream. Sprinkle with chives.

SERVES 4

SCALLION Crêpes

▸ **CRÊPES**

1/2 cup all-purpose flour

1/4 teaspoon salt

1/8 teaspoon pepper

2 eggs, lightly beaten

3/4 cup milk (or more if necessary)

1 tablespoon butter, melted

1 scallion (green onion), thinly sliced

Butter for cooking crêpes

▸ **FILLING**

2/3 cup light sour cream

3 ounces red (salmon) caviar

In a medium bowl, combine the flour, salt and pepper. Add the eggs and whisk until smooth. Gradually add milk, whisking until batter is free of lumps. Stir in melted butter and scallions. Cover and let batter rest for at least 20 minutes.

Heat a crêpe pan or small nonstick frying pan. Butter the pan very lightly. If needed, thin batter with milk so that it is the consistency of heavy cream. Use about 1/2 tablespoon of the batter for each crêpe, spreading to a 2" circle with the back of a spoon. Cook for about 1 minute on the first side, turn and cook for about 30 seconds.

To serve, use the crêpes at room temperature, or warm if you prefer. Put the crêpes on a work surface. Spread with about 3/4 teaspoon sour cream to 1/4" of edge. Cover with 1/2 teaspoon caviar and fold in half. Serve with champagne.

SERVES 10-12

Mini Bagel
PIZZAS

- 12 mini bagels, cut in half
  Tomato paste

- **FILLINGS**
  Pepperoni, sausage, anchovies, mushrooms,
  hamburger, smoked oysters, etc.

- **TOPPINGS**
  Mozzarella, Parmesan cheese, garlic powder, dried oregano

Preheat oven to 350°. Scoop out the soft centers of the bagels.
Place in oven to toast, 5-8 minutes. Remove toasted bagels
from oven and increase temperature to 375°.

Spread each bagel half with tomato paste, then with filling(s)
of your choice. Top with cheeses, garlic powder and oregano.
Cook in oven until cheese melts, about 10 minutes. Serve hot.

SERVES 12

DINNER
IN A DISH
IN A DASH

DINNER **IN A DISH IN A DASH**

Below many of the dinners is a suggested side dish… but feel free to mix and match!

SEAFOOD

POULTRY

BEEF AND MORE

Sea Bass

WITH CRACKED PEPPER BUTTER

> ▸ 2 cloves garlic
> 2 tablespoons unsalted butter, softened
> 2 teaspoons cracked black pepper
> 1 teaspoon prepared mustard
> 1/2 teaspoon salt
> Juice of 1 lemon
> 4 6-ounce sea bass fillets, dried well with paper towels

Preheat oven to 375°. In food processor fitted with steel blade, chop garlic. Add butter, pepper, mustard, salt and lemon juice and process to combine well. Place fish in baking pan. Spoon mound of butter on top of each piece of fish. Bake for 10-15 minutes or until done. Baste once or twice during baking.

Place 2 large spoonfuls of Tomato Parmesan Grits (facing page) on serving plate, centered, and place 1 piece of fish in center of grits. Serve with steamed sugar snap peas (or any green vegetable).

SERVES 4

Tomato Parmesan GRITS

▸ 3 cups water

1/4 teaspoon salt

1/4 cup quick-cooking grits

1 8-ounce can tomato sauce

1/4 cup grated Parmesan cheese
(or more, as desired)

Bring water to a boil. Add salt.
Add grits slowly, stirring constantly.
Reduce heat to simmer. Cover
and cook for 5-7 minutes, stirring
occasionally. When grits are done,
add tomato sauce and cheese;
stir thoroughly. Serve hot.

SERVES 4

Sea Bass
WITH VEGETABLES

▸ **SEA BASS**

4 6-ounce sea bass fillets

Salt and pepper to taste

2 tablespoons lemon oil
(Available in specialty food shops)

1 tablespoon vegetable oil

Salt and pepper to taste

Juice of 2 lemons

▸ **VEGETABLES**

2 onions, cut into 1" dice

2 large cloves garlic, minced

1 cup shiitake (or other) mushrooms, sliced

6-8 small red potatoes, cut into
quarters, boiled and drained

1/2 pound thin green beans,
asparagus or peas, blanched

4 tomatoes, quartered

12-15 fresh basil leaves, coarsely chopped

Season fish with salt and pepper. Spoon lemon oil over fish. In a large frying pan, heat the vegetable oil to medium-high and cook the fish 3-4 minutes on each side, depending on thickness of fish. Remove from pan and set aside.

In same pan used to cook fish, cook onions over medium heat (adding a little oil if needed) for about 5 minutes, or until they begin to soften. Add garlic and mushrooms. Cook for 3-4 minutes. Add cooked potatoes, tomatoes, green beans and basil; stir to heat through. Drizzle lemon juice over all. Season with salt and pepper to taste. Return fish to pan with vegetables and heat through. Serve hot.

SERVES 4

RAGOÛT

1 tablespoon olive oil

1 large onion, chopped

2 large cloves garlic, minced

1 28-ounce can tomatoes with juice

1 8-ounce can tomato paste

1 6-ounce can tomato sauce

1 cup water

1 tablespoon salt

1 tablespoon granulated sugar

1 teaspoon freshly ground black pepper

1/4 teaspoon red pepper flakes

Few drops hot sauce

2 tablespoons chopped fresh parsley

1 tablespoon chopped fresh oregano

1/4 cup chopped fresh basil

SEAFOOD

1 pound shrimp, shelled and deveined

1/2 pound bay scallops

1/2 pound mussels

1/2 pound clams

1 pound salmon fillets, cut into cubes

1 pound grouper, sea bass or halibut fillets, cut into cubes (see note)

Hot cooked rice or orzo pasta

Green peas for garnish

Catch of the Day
SEAFOOD
Ragoût

Heat oil in a large pot. Add onion and garlic; sauté until tender, about 5 minutes. Add tomatoes and juice, tomato paste, tomato sauce and water. Cover and simmer for about 15 minutes. Add salt, sugar, pepper, red pepper flakes, hot sauce, parsley, oregano and basil; simmer 5 minutes longer. Add shellfish and fish cubes. Simmer 3-5 minutes or until done.

Serve with rice or orzo pasta. Garnish with green peas.

NOTE: Any combination of firm-fleshed fish and/or shellfish may be used.

SERVES 4-6

Woven Salmon & Sea Bass
WITH DILL PESTO SAUCE

▸ **PESTO**

2 cloves garlic, peeled

1 large bunch fresh dill, stems removed

1/4 cup fresh parsley

2 tablespoons pinenuts (or pecans)

6 tablespoons grated Parmesan cheese

1 1/4 cups olive oil, divided

1 teaspoon salt

1 tablespoon granulated sugar

Freshly ground black pepper to taste

1/2 cup red wine vinegar

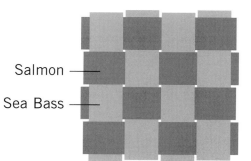

Salmon

Sea Bass

▸ **FISH**

1 pound salmon fillets, skin removed

1 pound sea bass fillets, skin removed

Salt and pepper to taste

Juice of 1 lemon

PESTO: Place garlic, dill, parsley, nuts and Parmesan in work bowl of food processor. Process until well combined. Add 1/4 cup of the oil through feed tube while machine is running. Add salt, sugar, pepper and vinegar; combine ingredients well. With machine running, slowly add remaining 1 cup oil through the feed tube. Set aside.

FISH: Preheat oven to 350°. Cut fillets into 1/2" by 5" strips. Weave strips basket-weave fashion (over and under, see diagram) into four 4" squares. Lift squares with a spatula and place in a baking dish. Season lightly with salt and pepper; drizzle with lemon juice. Cover baking dish with aluminum foil and bake for 10-15 minutes. To serve: place woven fish on serving plates and drizzle with Pesto Sauce. Serve with Corn and Black Bean Salad (facing page).

SERVES 4

Corn & Black Bean
SALAD

▶ **VEGETABLES**

Kernels cut from 4 ears corn,
blanched 5 minutes and drained

1 16-ounce can black beans,
rinsed and drained

2 tomatoes, seeded and diced

3 green onions, with tops, thinly sliced

1 cup Vinaigrette Dressing
(or more if needed)

▶ **VINAIGRETTE DRESSING**
(Yield: 1 1/2 cups)

1 clove garlic, minced

1 teaspoon Dijon mustard

1 teaspoon salt

1/8 teaspoon freshly ground black pepper

1 tablespoon granulated sugar

1/2 cup red wine vinegar

1 cup vegetable oil

Romaine or Boston lettuce leaves

VEGETABLES: In a large bowl, combine the corn, black beans, tomatoes and green onions.

VINAIGRETTE: Place garlic, mustard, salt, pepper, sugar and vinegar in work bowl of food processor. With machine running, slowly pour the oil through the feed tube in a steady stream.

Add vinaigrette dressing to vegetables and toss to combine well. Chill, covered, for 2 hours to overnight. Serve on lettuce leaves.

SERVES 4

Baked Salmon
WITH PINEAPPLE SALSA

▸ **SALSA**

1 20-ounce can crushed pineapple, drained (reserve juice)

1 large tomato, seeded and cut into small dice

1 red onion, chopped

4 green onions, with tops, thinly sliced

2 cloves garlic, minced

1/2 cup black beans, rinsed and drained

1/4 teaspoon cayenne pepper (or more to taste)

1 jalapeño pepper, seeded and chopped fine

2 teaspoons lemon extract

▸ **SALMON**

2 pounds fresh salmon (4-6 fillets)

Juice of 2 lemons

Salt and pepper to taste

SALSA: In a large bowl, combine drained pineapple, tomato, red onion, green onion, garlic, black beans, cayenne, jalapeño and lemon extract. Mix well. Add the reserved pineapple juice gradually, mixing gently, until desired consistency is reached. (Use all of the juice for a thin, more sauce-like salsa.) Set aside.

SALMON: Preheat oven to 350°. Place salmon in baking pan. Pour lemon juice over. Season with salt and pepper. Let marinate 10-15 minutes. Cover pan with aluminum foil. Bake 10-15 minutes, depending on thickness of salmon. Serve with Salsa and Orzo Primavera (facing page).

SERVES 4-6

ORZO
Primavera

▸ **ORZO**

2 cups cooked orzo pasta, well drained

2 small carrots, thinly sliced

1 red bell pepper, cored, seeded and diced

1 cup snow peas, cut in half at an angle

1 cup asparagus tips

1 cup Parmesan Dressing

▸ **PARMESAN DRESSING**
(Yield: about 2 cups)

1 clove garlic, minced

1 tablespoon Dijon mustard

1 teaspoon salt

1/8 teaspoon freshly ground black pepper

1 tablespoon granulated sugar

1/2 cup red wine vinegar

1/2 cup grated Parmesan cheese

1 cup vegetable oil

DRESSING: In work bowl of food processor, combine the garlic, mustard, salt, pepper, sugar, vinegar and Parmesan cheese. With machine running, pour the oil through the feed tube in a slow, steady stream.

ORZO: Place orzo in bowl. Add carrots and peppers. Steam snow peas and asparagus for 1-2 minutes. Cool and add to bowl. Toss to combine well. Add dressing. Mix well. Chill in refrigerator 2 hours or overnight.

SERVES 4-6

ORANGE-GLAZED Grouper

▸ **GROUPER**

4 5-ounce grouper fillets (see note)

Salt and pepper to taste

Juice of 1/2 lemon

Juice of 1/2 orange

1 tablespoon butter

Orange slices for garnish

3 green onions, thinly sliced, for garnish

▸ **GLAZE**

1/2 cup sweet orange marmalade

2 tablespoons orange juice

4 teaspoons orange liqueur

GLAZE: In a small pan, combine marmalade, orange juice and liqueur. Heat to warm; set aside.

GROUPER: Season fish with salt and pepper. Spoon lemon and orange juices over fish. Melt butter in large skillet over medium-high heat. Place fish in pan and cook 3-5 minutes, depending on thickness. Turn fish and cook for 5 minutes or until done. Spoon glaze over fish. Let glaze warm over fish for 1-2 minutes. Garnish with orange slices and sprinkle with sliced onions. Serve with Raisin Rice Salad (facing page).

NOTE: Substitute any firm-fleshed fish as desired — swordfish, sea bass, etc.

SERVES 4

Raisin
RICE SALAD

▶ **SALAD**

2/3 cup long-grain rice, cooked according to package directions

1/3 cup wild rice, cooked according to package directions

1/2 cup chopped sweet onions (Vidalias, red or both)

1/2 cup fresh English peas, blanched (or frozen, thawed but not cooked)

1/4 cup chopped celery

1/4 cup chopped carrots

1/4 cup white raisins

▶ **DRESSING**

1 clove garlic

1 teaspoon Dijon mustard

1 teaspoon salt

1/4 teaspoon freshly ground black pepper

1 tablespoon granulated sugar

1 teaspoon dried thyme

1/2 cup red wine vinegar

1 cup light olive oil

DRESSING: Chop garlic in work bowl of food processor fitted with a steel blade. Add mustard, salt, pepper, sugar, thyme and vinegar. Add oil through feed tube in a slow, steady stream.

SALAD: In a large bowl, combine rices, onions, peas, celery, carrots and raisins. Add 1/2 cup of the dressing and toss to mix well. Add more dressing as desired.

SERVES 6

Grilled Fish
KEBABS

▸ **MARINADE**

1/2 cup soy sauce

1/2 cup dark sesame oil

Juice of 1 lemon

2 cloves garlic, minced

1 teaspoon freshly ground black pepper

▸ **FISH**

1/2 pound tuna fillet, 1" thick, cut into 4 cubes

1/2 pound salmon fillet, 1" thick, cut into 4 cubes

1/2 pound sea bass fillet, 1" thick, cut into 4 cubes

12 large raw shrimp, peeled and deveined

▸ **KEBABS**

2 large red bell peppers, cored, seeded and cut into 1" chunks

2 medium red onions, cut into 1" chunks

4 wooden skewers

MARINADE: In a small bowl, whisk together the soy sauce, sesame oil, lemon juice, garlic and pepper.

FISH: Place fish cubes and shrimp in a nonreactive (glass or stainless steel) dish with sides. Spoon marinade over fish and shrimp. Cover and refrigerate for 1-2 hours. Meanwhile, soak wooden skewers in water 1-2 hours.

KEBABS: Prepare skewers in this order (reserving fish marinade):
1 piece tuna, pepper and onion;
1 piece salmon, pepper and onion;
1 piece sea bass, pepper and onion;
3 shrimp, pepper and onion. Place filled skewers on hot grill, 4-5 minutes per side, brushing each side with marinade as kebabs cook. Turn once.

Place remaining marinade in a small saucepan and cook over low heat for about 5 minutes. Serve kebabs over Fresh Corn and Tomatoes (facing page) and spoon marinade over fish.

SERVES 4

Fresh Corn
AND TOMATOES

▸ 2 tablespoons butter

1 onion, diced

Kernels cut from 4 ears corn

2 tomatoes, diced

Salt and pepper to taste

Chopped chives

Melt butter in a medium skillet. Over medium heat, add onion and sauté until softened, about 5 minutes. Add corn and tomatoes, season with salt and pepper and continue to cook for 4-5 minutes or until done. Sprinkle with chopped chives.

SERVES 4

TUNA
Burgers

- 1 pound tuna fillets
- 2 cloves garlic, minced
- 3 tablespoons Dijon mustard
- 1/4 teaspoon Cayenne pepper
- 1 teaspoon salt
- 1/4 teaspoon freshly ground black pepper
- 2 tablespoons vegetable oil
- 4 sesame seed buns
- Hot Chinese mustard
- Teriyaki barbecue sauce

Chop the tuna with a large sharp knife or grind in a meat grinder to the texture of hamburger meat. (Do not use a food processor, which would shred the tuna, not chop it.) Place the tuna in a large bowl and add the garlic, mustard, cayenne, salt and pepper; mix thoroughly. Divide the mixture into 4 equal portions. Using your hands (moisten them with cold water for ease of handling), roll each portion into a smooth ball. Flatten each ball into a patty about 1" thick.

Heat the oil in a large skillet over medium-high heat and sear the burgers until they are browned and medium (or to desired degree of doneness), 3-4 minutes per side.

Place burgers on heated buns spread with hot Chinese mustard and/or teriyaki barbecue sauce. Serve with Potato Tomato Soup (facing page).

SERVES 4

Potato Tomato
SOUP

▸ 2 tablespoons butter

1 large onion, cut into 1" dice

2 large baking potatoes, peeled and cut into 1" dice

4 large cloves garlic, peeled and left whole

4 cups chicken stock, homemade if available, or canned

1 14-ounce can diced tomatoes, drained

2 teaspoons salt

Freshly ground black pepper to taste

Shredded cheddar or Asiago cheese for garnish

Chopped chives for garnish

Melt butter in a stockpot over medium heat. Add onions and sauté until they begin to soften, stirring occasionally, about 5 minutes. Add potatoes, garlic and stock; lower heat, cover and simmer until potatoes are done, about 15 minutes. Puree potato mixture in work bowl of food processor fitted with steel blade. Return purée to stockpot over low heat. Add tomatoes, salt and pepper. Simmer for 2-3 minutes. Taste and adjust seasoning. Garnish with cheese and chives. Serve hot.

NOTE: If soup is too thick, thin with chicken stock.

SERVES 4

Seared Tuna
WITH ASIAN-STYLE PASTA

▸ **DRESSING**

1/2 cup dark sesame oil

1/2 cup soy sauce

1 clove garlic, minced

1/4 teaspoon freshly ground black pepper

2 tablespoons rice wine vinegar

1 tablespoon prepared Thai peanut sauce

▸ **PASTA**

8 ounces penne pasta, cooked according to package directions

1 red bell pepper, cored, seeded and cut into strips

3 green onions, thinly sliced

1/4 cup chopped cashews

▸ **TUNA**

4 6-ounce tuna fillets

Salt and pepper

Juice of 1 lemon

1 tablespoon dark sesame oil

1/4 cup prepared hoisin sauce

DRESSING: In a medium bowl, whisk together the sesame oil, soy sauce, garlic, pepper, vinegar and peanut sauce. Set aside.

PASTA: In a large bowl, combine pasta, pepper strips, green onions and cashews. Toss with half the dressing; reserve remaining dressing.

TUNA: Season tuna lightly with salt and pepper. Drizzle lemon juice over fish. In a 12" skillet, heat oil to medium-high. Cook tuna 2-3 minutes. Turn fish with a spatula. Spoon hoisin sauce evenly over fish. Continue to cook 3-4 minutes, depending on thickness of fish.

TO SERVE: Divide pasta onto 4 serving plates. Place tuna, sliced or whole, on pasta. Drizzle with reserved dressing.

SERVES 4

SHRIMP
Salad Niçoise

▸ **SALAD**

Red-tipped or green leaf lettuce or field greens

6-8 large shrimp, cooked, peeled and deveined

2 or 3 new (red) potatoes, quarted and cooked

6-8 thin green beans, blanched

1 hard-boiled egg, quartered

1 Roma tomato, sliced

4 or 5 black olives

Red and yellow bell pepper strips (optional)

Red onion rings (optional)

Remoulade Sauce

▸ **REMOULADE SAUCE**
(Yield 1 1/2 cups)

1 cup mayonnaise

1/4 cup prepared dill pickle relish

1 tablespoon chopped capers

1 teaspoon Dijon mustard

2 teaspoons anchovy paste

1 tablespoon chopped fresh parsley

1/2 teaspoon dried tarragon

1/2 cup chili sauce

REMOULADE SAUCE: Whisk together the mayonnaise, pickle relish, capers, mustard, anchovy paste, parsley, tarragon and chili sauce. Store in refrigerator.

SALAD: Place lettuce on serving plate or in a bowl. Attractively arrange shrimp, potatoes, beans, egg quarters, tomato slices and olives on lettuce. Garnish with pepper strips and onion rings, if desired. Drizzle with Remoulade Sauce.

SERVES 1

MACADAMIA-CRUSTED
Chicken Breasts

▸ 4 boneless, skinless chicken breast halves
Salt and pepper to taste
4 tablespoons sharp-flavored honey mustard
1/2 cup finely chopped macadamia nuts (see note)
1 tablespoon light olive oil

Preheat oven to 375°. Season chicken breasts with salt and pepper. Using a spoon, coat the "skin-side" of each breast with 1 tablespoon honey mustard. With your fingers, press 2 tablespoons chopped nuts onto each breast. Heat oil in an ovenproof skillet. Over medium heat, brown uncoated side of chicken 3-4 minutes. Do not turn. Place skillet in oven and bake for 8-10 minutes or until firm to the touch. Serve hot or at room temperature with Mixed Vegetable Ragoût (facing page).

NOTE: Pecans, almonds or walnuts may be substituted.

SERVES 4-6

MIXED VEGETABLE
Ragoût

▸ 1 tablespoon canola oil

1 onion, diced

6-8 cloves garlic, whole

2 zucchini, cut into chunks

2 yellow squash, cut into chunks

2 tomatoes, cut into chunks

1 cup yellow corn kernels, cut fresh from cob or frozen

Salt and pepper to taste

1/2 cup prepared vinaigrette dressing

Heat oil in a large pan. Add onion and garlic cloves.
Cook over medium heat, stirring often, until onion
and garlic begin to soften, 4-5 minutes. Add zucchini,
yellow squash, tomatoes and corn. Cook, stirring
occasionally, 6-8 minutes. Season with salt and pepper.
Add dressing, mix well. Cook 2-3 minutes longer.
Taste for seasoning. Serve hot or at room temperature.

SERVES 4-6

MARINATED
Basil Chicken Breasts

- 4 boneless, skinless chicken breast halves
  1/4 cup plus 2 tablespoons light olive oil, divided
  2 cloves garlic, minced
  1 cup fresh basil leaves, chopped
  Juice of 1 lemon
  1 teaspoon salt
  1/4 teaspoon freshly ground black pepper

Place chicken breasts in a nonreactive dish. In a medium bowl, whisk together 1/4 cup olive oil, garlic, basil, lemon juice, salt and pepper until well combined. Spoon marinade over chicken, cover and place in refrigerator for 1 hour or longer (can be prepared to this point the day before).

Remove chicken from refrigerator 30 minutes before cooking. Heat 2 tablespoons oil in large skillet to medium heat. Place chicken in skillet and cook 4-5 minutes on each side or until firm to the touch. Slice and place in "fan" on serving plates. Serve with Barley Salad (facing page).

SERVES 4

Barley
SALAD

▸ **SALAD**

2 cups chicken stock

1 cup fine barley

2 carrots, shredded

3 green onions, thinly sliced

3/4 cup Vinaigrette Dressing

Salt and pepper to taste

Green lettuce leaves

▸ **VINAIGRETTE DRESSING**
(Yield: 1 1/2 cups)

1 clove garlic, minced

1 teaspoon Dijon mustard

1 teaspoon salt

1/8 teaspoon freshly ground black pepper

1 tablespoon granulated sugar

1/2 cup red wine vinegar

1 cup vegetable or canola oil

In a saucepan over medium heat, bring stock to a boil. Add barley, reduce heat to low, cover and simmer for about 25 minutes. Place in a bowl to cool. Add carrots, onions and dressing. Toss to combine well. Taste for seasoning. Add salt and pepper if desired. Chill for at least 1 hour. Serve on a bed of green lettuce leaves.

Place garlic, mustard, salt, pepper, sugar and vinegar in work bowl of food processor. With machine running, pour the oil through the feed tube in a slow steady stream.

SERVES 4

Pan-Grilled CHICKEN
with Ratatouille Pasta

▸ 4 boneless, skinless chicken breast halves

4 boneless, skinless chicken thighs

Salt and freshly ground black pepper to taste

2 teaspoons garlic powder

2 teaspoons dried oregano

2 tablespoons canola oil

Season chicken pieces with salt, pepper, garlic powder and oregano. Heat the oil in a large skillet to medium high. Cook chicken 6-7 minutes on each side or until done. Remove from pan and keep warm.

Place a large spoonful of the Ratatouille Pasta (facing page) on a serving plate. Top with a chicken breast and thigh. Garnish with sliced cheese and additional chopped basil or parsley, if desired.

SERVES 4

Ratatouille PASTA

- 1 tablespoon canola oil
- 2 or more cloves garlic, minced
- 1 large onion, sliced
- 2 zucchini, cut in 1" cubes
- 1 small eggplant, peeled and cut in 1" cubes
- 3 tablespoons all-purpose flour
- 1 red bell pepper, cored, seeded and cut in 1/4" strips
- 1 yellow bell pepper, cored, seeded and cut in 1/4" strips
- 4-5 tomatoes, diced
- 1 tablespoon capers
- 12 leaves fresh basil, chopped
- 8 ounces rotelle or rotini pasta, cooked according to package directions and drained

Thinly sliced Parmesan or Asiago cheese for garnish
Additional chopped basil or parsely for garnish (optional)

Reheat same skillet from Pan-Grilled Chicken (facing page) with drippings and oil to medium. Add garlic and onion and cook until onion is transparent, 4-5 minutes. Dredge zucchini and eggplant pieces in flour, shake off excess flour and add to skillet. Cover and cook slowly for about 10 minutes. Add the peppers and tomatoes and simmer, uncovered, until mixture thickens, 6-8 minutes. Season with salt and pepper. Add the capers, basil and pasta and mix throughly.

NOTE: While this dish is great with the Pan-Grilled Chicken, it's just as good on its own!

SERVES 4

Chicken Osso Bucco

▸ **CHICKEN**

1/2 cup all-purpose flour

1 teaspoon salt

1/4 teaspoon pepper

4 chicken thighs

4 chicken legs

2 tablespoons vegetable oil

▸ **GREMOLATA**

3 tablespoons chopped parsley

1 tablespoon grated lemon rind

1 teaspoon minced garlic

▸ **SAUCE**

1/2 cup chopped onion

1 cup chopped celery

1 cup sliced carrots

2 cloves garlic, minced

1 cup dry white wine

1 8-ounce can tomato sauce

1 tablespoon chopped fresh basil

1 teaspoon dried thyme

8 ounces spaghetti, cooked according to package directions and drained

CHICKEN: Combine flour, salt and pepper. Coat chicken pieces with flour mixture. Heat oil in a large skillet over medium-high heat. Add chicken and brown on both sides. Remove chicken; set aside.

SAUCE: In same skillet used to cook chicken, add onion and cook until tender, about 5 minutes. Add celery, carrots, minced garlic cloves, wine, tomato sauce, basil and thyme. Return chicken to skillet. Cover, reduce heat to low and simmer 25-30 minutes.

GREMOLATA: In a small bowl, combine the parsley, lemon rind and minced garlic.

TO SERVE: sprinkle gremolata over chicken. Serve over hot, cooked spaghetti.

SERVES 4

Chicken with Spuds
AND GREEN BEANS

- 1 frying chicken, 2 1/2 to 3 pounds, cut into serving pieces
  Salt and pepper
  1-2 tablespoons oil for frying chicken
  2 Yukon Gold or Idaho potatoes, peeled and cut into 1" cubes
  2 onions, diced
  3 cloves garlic, minced
  1 cup white wine
  1 14-ounce can diced tomatoes with juice
  1 teaspoon dried oregano
  3/4 pound fresh green beans, cut into 1" pieces and blanched for 5 minutes and drained

Season chicken pieces with salt and pepper. Heat oil in a large skillet and brown chicken well. Remove from skillet and set aside. In same pan, brown potatoes, onions and garlic. Return chicken to skillet with potatoes. Add wine and tomatoes. Sprinkle with oregano. Cover and simmer gently for 20-25 minutes. Add green beans. Simmer 5 minutes longer. Taste and adjust for seasoning.

SERVES 3-4

CHICKEN NAPOLEON

- 4 boneless, skinless chicken breast halves, flattened with a meat pounder

  Salt and pepper to taste

  2 cloves garlic, minced

  1 tablespoon olive oil

  1 tablespoon chopped fresh basil

  1 tablespoon fresh oregano

  4 slices (1/2" thick) tomato

  4 slices (1/2" thick) eggplant

  4 slices (1/2" thick) red onion

4 slices (1/2" thick) red bell pepper rings

4 slices (1/2" thick) yellow bell pepper rings

1 8-ounce bottle prepared vinaigrette dressing

4 oz. chèvre (goat cheese), crumbled

3-4 tablespoons vegetable oil (as needed) for cooking vegetables

4 tablespoons oil-packed sun-dried tomatoes, drained and chopped

1/2 cup pinenuts

Season chicken breasts with salt and pepper; place in shallow dish. Spread with garlic, brush with olive oil and sprinkle with basil and oregano. Place in refrigerator to marinate for about 1 hour. Place vegetable slices in another shallow dish and pour vinaigrette dressing over. Let marinate.

In a large frying pan, heat vegetable oil and sauté chicken breasts 2-3 minutes on each side. Remove to 4 serving plates and keep warm.

In same pan, sauté vegetable slices, in order listed, in a little of the vinaigrette dressing. (Eggplant, onions and peppers will take longer than the tomatoes.) Beginning with tomatoes, stack vegetable slices on cooked chicken breasts in order given. Garnish with bits of goat cheese, pieces of sun-dried tomatoes and pinenuts. Serve with Garden Vegetable Cousous (facing page).

SERVES 4

GARDEN VEGETABLE
Couscous

- 1 10-ounce box couscous, prepared according to package directions, cooled and fluffed with a fork

  1 cucumber, diced

  1 tomato, seeded and diced

  3 green onions, thinly sliced

  1/2 cup diced celery

  4 radishes, diced

  1/2 cup prepared vinaigrette dressing, or more if needed

  Crumbled goat cheese (optional)

Place prepared couscous in a bowl. Add cucumber, tomato, onions, celery and radishes. Pour in dressing and mix well. Chill until ready to serve. Add small bits of goat cheese if desired.

SERVES 4

LIME
Roast Chicken

- 1 whole frying chicken, 3 to 3 1/2 pounds, butterflied
  1 lime
  2 cloves garlic, minced
  Salt and pepper
  3-4 tablespoons lime preserves or marmalade
  Lime slices for garnish

Preheat oven to 400°. Using poultry scissors, cut chicken on both sides of backbone; remove bone. Gently pull chicken out flat while holding both wings. Place chicken on open roasting pan (cookie sheet with 1" sides will work) and gently press down on breast bone to cause chicken to lie as flat as possible. Squeeze juice of 1 lime over chicken, rub with garlic and season with salt and pepper. Place in oven for 45-50 minutes. Remove chicken from oven and spoon lime marmalade over chicken, making sure that the entire surface is covered with marmalade. Return to oven and cook 10-15 minutes longer. Cut into quarters and serve. Garnish with lime slices. Serve with Pan Potatoes, Onions and Mushrooms (facing page).

NOTE: For a more intense lime flavor, place 2-3 lime slices under the skin of the chicken, at the breast.

SERVES 4

PAN POTATOES,
Onions and Mushrooms

▸ 2 tablespoons butter

2 tablespoons light olive oil

2 onions, coarsely chopped

3 large russet or Yukon Gold potatoes, cut into 1" cubes

2 cups sliced shiitake mushrooms

Salt, pepper and garlic powder to taste

In a large frying pan, melt the butter and heat the oilve oil over medium heat. Add onions and cook for 5 minutes, stirring once or twice. Add potatoes, mix well with onions, cover, lower heat, and cook for 15-20 minutes, stirring as needed until potatoes begin to soften. Add mushrooms, mix well and cook, uncovered, for 6-8 minutes longer, stirring occasionally. Season with salt, pepper and garlic powder. Mix well. Serve hot.

SERVES 4

Apricot-Glazed
Cornish Hens
with Pistachio Rice

- ▸ 2 tablespoons butter, divided
  3/4 cup apricot preserves
  4 Cornish hens
  1 cup white raisins
  3 tablespoons brandy
  1/4 cup shallots, minced
  1/2 cup pistachio nuts
  1 package long grain and wild rice mix, prepared according to package directions

Preheat oven to 375°.

In a saucepan, combine 1 tablespoon butter and preserves. Melt until syrupy; set aside.

Roast hens, uncovered for 1 hour. During the last 10-15 minutes of cooking, spoon apricot glaze over hens. Meanwhile, soak raisins in brandy for 15 minutes. Saute shallots in 1 tablespoon butter until lightly browned. Add drained raisins, shallots and nuts to hot cooked rice. Serve hens over hot rice (or rice can be served separately) with Roasted Asparagus (facing page).

SERVES 4

ROASTED Asparagus

- 1 bunch asparagus (about 1 pound)
  1 tablespoon vegetable oil
  Salt and pepper
  Juice of 1 lemon

Preheat broiler. Break off the tough ends of asparagus. Peel the stalks. Place asparagus in a single layer on a baking pan. Drizzle oil over all, making sure to cover all the stalks well. Sprinkle with a little salt and pepper. Place pan under broiler for 2-3 minutes. Check for doneness (asparagus should be tender crisp). If not done, broil for 1-2 minutes longer. Remove pan from broiler; drizzle with lemon juice. Serve hot.

SERVES 4

Chicken
IN THE POT

- 1 whole chicken, 3 1/2 to 4 pounds
  1 onion, peeled and left whole
  2 carrots, peeled and thinly sliced
  2 ribs celery, thinly sliced
  2 10-ounce cans chicken broth
  1 14-ounce can diced tomatoes, with juice (optional)
  1 tablespoon salt
  1/4 teaspoon freshly ground black pepper
  1 teaspoon dried thyme
  1 teaspoon garlic powder
  2 to 3 quarts water to cover chicken
  4 ounces fine noodles, broken into small pieces
  English peas (optional)

Place chicken in a large stockpot (8 quarts) with onion, carrots, celery, chicken broth, tomatoes (if using), salt, pepper, thyme, garlic powder and water. Bring to a boil over high heat, skimming off any foam that may accumulate. Cover pot, reduce heat to low and simmer for 1 1/4 to 1 1/2 hours. Remove chicken from pot. Let cool. When cool enough to handle, remove chicken from bones. Discard skin and bones. Cut meat into bite-size pieces and return to pot. Add noodles and simmer for 10 minutes. Serve in bowls. English peas may be added, if desired.

SERVES 4-6

TURKEY CUTLETS Cacciatore

- 1 tablespoon light olive oil
- 1 pound turkey breast cutlets
- Salt and pepper to taste
- 1 onion, diced
- 1 rib celery, finely diced
- 2 carrots, finely diced
- 2 cloves garlic, minced
- 1 8-ounce can tomato sauce
- 1/2 cup white wine
- 1/2 cup chicken stock, canned or homemade
- 15 fresh basil leaves, chopped
- 1/4 cup fresh parsley, chopped
- A few drops of hot sauce
- Hot cooked rice

Heat oil in a large skillet over medium-high heat. Season cutlets with salt and pepper. Brown cutlets on both sides. Remove from pan and set aside.

In same skillet, sauté onions until they begin to soften, 3-4 minutes. Add celery and carrots and cook, stirring occasionally, 5 minutes longer. Add garlic, tomato sauce, wine and stock. Simmer 5 minutes or until vegetables are done. Add basil, parsley, hot sauce and salt and pepper to taste. Simmer 1-2 minutes longer. Return turkey cutlets to skillet with sauce. Simmer 5-6 minutes or until heated through. Serve over hot cooked rice.

SERVES 2-3

TURKEY
Veggie Burgers

▸ 1 pound ground turkey

1 teaspoon salt

1/8 teaspoon freshly ground black pepper

1 clove garlic, minced

1/2 cup shredded carrots

12 spinach leaves, coarsely chopped

6 fresh basil leaves, coarsely chopped

1 tablespoon light oil

3-4 buns

Place ground turkey in a mixing bowl. Add salt, pepper, garlic, carrots, spinach and basil leaves. Mix well with hands and form into 3 large or 4 smaller burgers.

In a large skillet, heat olive oil to medium-high. Add burgers and cook 3-4 minutes. Turn burgers and continue to cook for 3-4 minutes. Serve plain or on buns with mustard and ketchup (as desired) and with Fit Fries (facing page).

SERVES 3-4

Fit Fries
(LOW-FAT OVEN FRIES)

▸ Nonstick cooking spray
  2 large Idaho potaoes, peeled and cut into 1/4" strips
  1 tablespoon light olive oil
  Kosher salt

Preheat oven to 375°. Spray a 10"x15" baking sheet with cooking spray. Place potatoes on pan and drizzle oil over; toss to coat. Bake 30-40 minutes. Sprinkle with salt. Serve hot.

SERVES 3-4

QUICK & HEALTHY
Turkey Wraps

- 4 flour tortillas (9" diameter)
- 1 cup shredded extra-sharp cheddar cheese
- 12 slices deli-style turkey, about 1/2 pound, or use leftover turkey
- 1 cup seeded and diced tomatoes
- 1 cup rinsed and drained canned black beans
- 4 tablespoons prepared hot salsa
- 1 cup shredded iceberg or romaine lettuce
- Nonfat cooking spray

Place the tortillas on a cutting board or other flat surface. Sprinkle 1/4 cup of the cheese on each. Layer 3 slices turkey over the cheese. Add 1/4 cup tomatoes to each, followed by 1/4 cup black beans. Spread 1 tablespoon salsa over beans and top with 1/4 cup lettuce. Roll tortillas, jellyroll-style, ending with seam underneath.

Spray a 12" skillet with cooking spray. Heat pan to medium and place tortillas, seam side down, in pan. Allow them to cook for 2-3 minutes on each side, turning once, or until cheese has melted and ingredients are heated through. Serve with Matchstick Jicama Salad (facing page).

SERVES 2

Matchstick
JICAMA SALAD

▶ SALAD

1 small jicama bulb, about 1/2 pound,
cut into matchstick-size pieces, 2" long

1 carrot, cut into matchstick-size pieces

1/2 red bell pepper, cut
into matchstick-size pieces

1/2 yellow bell pepper, cut
into matchstick-size pieces

1/2 red onion, cut into
matchstick-size pieces

3 green onions, sliced

Red Pepper Dressing

▶ RED PEPPER DRESSING
(Yield: 1 1/2 cups)

1 clove garlic

1 red bell pepper, cored, seeded
and cut into chunks

3 green onions, cut into chunks

1 teaspoon salt

1/4 teaspoon freshly ground black pepper

1 tablespoon granulated sugar

1/2 cup red wine vinegar

1 cup canola oil

SALAD: In a large bowl, combine the jicama, carrots, red and yellow peppers and onions. Toss well with Red Pepper Dressing.

DRESSING: Place garlic, red pepper, onions, salt, pepper, sugar and vinegar in blender container. Add oil slowly while machine is running.

SERVES 4

PICNIC
Steaks

- ▸ 4 8-ounce strip sirloin steaks
  Salt
  Freshly ground black pepper
  Garlic powder
  1 tablespoon vegetable oil

Season steaks with salt, pepper and garlic powder to taste.

Heat oil in a large skillet to medium-high. Cook steaks
3-4 minutes on each side, or to desired degree of doneness.
Remove from pan and let steaks rest for 5 minutes. Slice and
serve fan-style around Balsamic Potato Salad (facing page).

NOTE: Great for the grill!

SERVES 4

BALSAMIC
Potato Salad

- 1 pound new potatoes, cut into eighths and cooked in lightly salted boiling water until tender

  1/2 cup chopped celery

  2 tomatoes, seeded and diced

  1/2 pound green beans, cut into 1" pieces and blanched 5 minutes

  2-3 large dill pickles, finely chopped

  1 cup Balsamic Vinaigrette Dressing

- **BALSAMIC VINAIGRETTE**
  (Yield: about 1 3/4 cups)

  1 clove garlic

  1 teaspoon Dijon Mustard

  1 teaspoon salt

  1/4 teaspoon freshly ground black pepper

  1 tablespoon granulated sugar

  1/2 cup balsamic vinegar

  1 cup canola oil

SALAD: In a large bowl, combine cooked potatoes, celery, tomatoes, green beans and pickles. Add dressing and toss to combine well. Chill until ready to serve.

VINAIGRETTE: In work bowl of food processor fitted with steel blade, drop in garlic clove and chop. Add mustard, salt, pepper, sugar and vinegar. With machine running, slowly add oil through feed tube; combine well.

SERVES 4

Petite Filet Mignon
WITH BOW-TIE PASTA AND VEGGIES

▸ **STEAKS**

4 filets of beef, 4-5 ounces each,
cut 1 to 1 1/2" thick

Salt and freshly ground
black pepper to taste

2 cloves garlic, minced

2 tablespoons light olive oil

▸ **PASTA AND VEGGIES**

2 tablespoons vegetable oil

2 onions, cut in 1" dice

1 cup shiitake mushrooms, sliced

4 tomatoes cut into medium chunks

2 zucchini, cut into small chunks

2 tablespoons balsamic vinegar

2 teaspoons chopped fresh oregano
(or 1 teaspoon dried)

Salt and pepper to taste

8 ounces bow-tie pasta, cooked
according to package directions
and drained

1/2 cup grated Asiago or
Parmesan cheese

2 tablespoons chopped fresh parsely

STEAKS: Bring filets to room temperature before cooking. Season with salt and pepper and spread with garlic. Heat olive oil in a large skillet. Over medium-high heat, cook filets 2-3 minutes on each side for rare. Remove steaks from pan; set aside.

PASTA AND VEGGIES: In same skillet used to cook steaks, heat vegetable oil to medium. Add onions and cook until they begin to soften, about 5 minutes, stirring occasionally. Add mushrooms and tomatoes; continue to cook and stir until tomatoes begin to soften, 3-4 minutes. Add zucchini, vinegar, oregano, salt and pepper. Cook 1-2 minutes. Add pasta; stir to combine. Return filets to skillet. Heat through.

Divide hot steaks and pasta and veggies onto 4 plates. Garnish with cheese and parsely.

SERVES 4

Veal Medallions
ON LINGUINE

- ▸ 2 tenderloins of veal, 3/4 to 1 pound each
- Salt and pepper to taste
- Garlic powder
- 2 tablespoons vegetable oil
- 1/4 cup brandy or cognac
- 4 shallots, chopped
- 1/2 cup chicken broth
- 2 tablespoons cream
- 2 tomatoes, seeded and diced
- 12 fresh basil leaves, chopped
- 1 teaspoon dried thyme
- 8 ounces linguine pasta, cooked according to package directions and drained
- Chopped parsley for garnish

Slice each tenderloin into 6-8 medallions (3/4" thick). Season with salt, pepper and garlic powder. Heat oil in a large skillet to medium-high. Brown slices briefly on both sides, 2 minutes per side. Remove from pan, set aside and keep warm. Deglaze skillet with brandy. Ignite. Add shallots and sauté over medium heat 2-3 minutes. Add chicken broth and cream. Simmer for 1-2 minutes. Add tomatoes, basil and thyme; simmer for 2-3 minutes. Taste and adjust seasonings. Return veal to sauce in skillet, including any juices that have accumulated. Heat through and serve over hot pasta. Sprinkle with parsley and serve with thin green beans or vegetables of your choice.

SERVES 4-6

Lemon
VEAL CHOPS

- ▸ 4 one inch-thick veal chops (1" thick)
  Salt and pepper
  Juice and rind of 2 lemons
  2 tablespoons butter
  1 teaspoon dried oregano
  4 cloves garlic, sliced
  Lemon slices and Italian parsley for garnish

Season chops with salt and pepper. Drizzle juice of 1 lemon over chops. Melt butter in skillet. Over medium-high heat, sauté chops until golden brown, 5-6 minutes. Turn chops, drizzle with juice of remaining lemon, sprinkle with lemon rind and oregano. Add garlic slices to pan and cook 5-6 minutes or until done. Garnish with cooked garlic slices, lemon slices and parsley. Serve with Jumbo Potato Pancake (facing page) and steamed broccoli florets mixed with steamed and buttered baby carrots.

SERVES 4

JUMBO
Potato Pancake

▸ 3 large Idaho potatoes
  1 tablespoon butter
  1 tablespoon vegetable oil
  2 teaspoons salt

Preheat oven to 350°. Peel potatoes. Shred on large-hole side of hand grater or on grating blade of food processor. Melt butter with oil in a 12" ovenproof skillet and heat to medium. Place grated potatoes in pan and spread them to cover entire surface. Sprinkle with 1 teaspoon salt. Let cook until browned on bottom, 5-6 minutes. Turn pancake, using 2 large spatulas. Sprinkle with remaining salt. Cook on second side until lightly browned, about 5 minutes. Place pan in oven and bake until done, about 15 minutes. Cut into 4 wedges and serve hot.

SERVES 4

VEAL
Mini Meatloaves

▸ 1 pound ground veal

1 teaspoon salt

1/4 teaspoon freshly ground black pepper

1/4 cup finely chopped onions

2 cloves garlic, minced

1 slice rye bread soaked in 1/4 cup water

1/4 cup oil-packed sun-dried tomatoes, drained and coarsely chopped

8-10 shiitake mushrooms, coarsely chopped

1 egg

Ketchup or barbecue sauce (optional)

Preheat oven to 400°. In a large bowl, combine the veal, salt, pepper, onions, garlic, bread (with water), sun-dried tomatoes, mushrooms and egg. Using your hands, mix well. If mixture seems dry, add 1-2 tablespoons water. Shape into 4 meatloaves. Place in baking dish or pan. Bake for 15-20 minutes. Top with ketchup or barbecue sauce, if desired. Serve with Baked Mashed Potatoes (facing page) and steamed English peas, if desired.

SERVES 4

Baked
MASHED POTATOES

▸ 3 or 4 russet or Yukon Gold potatoes, peeled and cut into cubes
Cold water to cover potatoes
2-3 tablespoons butter
1/4 cup milk
2-3 teaspoons salt

Preheat oven to 350°. Place potatoes in saucepan; add cold water to cover.
Cook over medium heat until soft, about 15 minutes. Drain potatoes and place
immediately into bowl of an electric mixer. Add butter, milk and salt and mix
until potatoes are smooth and lumps have disappeared. Place potatoes into
a well-greased 2-quart baking dish (use nonstick cooking spray or butter).
Place in oven and bake 20-30 minutes, or until potatoes begin to brown.

SERVES 4

Lamb Chops
WITH BLACK & WHITE BEAN RAGOÛT

▸ 8 lamb chops (1" thick)
   Salt and pepper to taste
   2 tablespoons Dijon mustard
   4 cloves garlic, minced
   1 tablespoon vegetable oil

Season chops with salt and pepper. Spread mustard and 4 cloves garlic on both sides of chops. Allow chops to marinate 1-2 hours or overnight, covered, in refrigerator. Remove chops from refrigerator 30 minutes before cooking. Heat 1 tablespoon oil in a large skillet to medium-high. Cook chops 3-4 minutes on each side.

To serve, divide Black & White Bean Ragoût (facing page) onto 4 serving plates. Place lamb chops over hot Ragoût. (Or as an alternative, serve over hash brown potatoes with onions.)

SERVES 4

Black & White Bean
RAGOÛT

- 1 tablespoon vegetable oil
- 1 onion diced
- 3 cloves garlic, minced
- 2 16-ounce cans white (cannellini) beans, rinsed and drained
- 1 16-ounce can black beans, rinsed and drained
- 1 14-ounce can diced tomatoes with juice
- 1/2 teaspoon salt
- 1/4 teaspoon freshly ground pepper
- 12 fresh basil leaves, chopped
- 1/2 cup oil-packed sun-dried tomatoes, drained and cut into small pieces
- 1/2 cup chicken stock (if needed)

In a large saucepan, heat 1 tablespoon oil over medium heat. Add the onion and garlic and cook, stirring frequently until onions begin to soften, about 5 minutes. Add white beans, black beans, tomatoes, salt, pepper, basil and sun-dried tomatoes. Stir to mix well, bring to a low boil, reduce heat and simmer for about 5 minutes. For a juicier ragoût, add 1/2 cup chicken stock. Taste and adjust seasoning.

SERVES 4

JAILHOUSE
Black Bean
CHILI DOG
Chili

▶ 1 tablespoon vegetable oil

1 large onion, diced

2 cloves garlic, minced

1 1/2 pounds lean ground chuck or round steak

1 14 1/2-ounce can diced tomatoes with juice

1/2 6 ounce can tomato paste

1/4 cup chili powder

1 teaspoon salt, or to taste

1/8 teaspoon freshly ground black pepper

A few drops hot sauce

1 tablespoon Worcestershire sauce

1 16-ounce can black beans, rinsed and drained

5 all-beef hot dogs, sliced into 1" chunks

Shredded sharp cheddar cheese (optional)

Heat oil in large skillet or stockpot. Add onion and garlic. Stirring occasionally, cook until wilted, about 5 minutes. Add ground beef and cook until browned, stirring frequently. Add tomatoes, tomato paste, chili powder, salt, pepper, hot sauce and Worcestershire. Stir to mix well, cover pan, reduce heat and simmer for about 20 minutes. Add beans and hot dogs and simmer for 10 minutes longer. Ladle hot chili into bowls and garnish with shredded cheese, if desired. Serve with House Salad (facing page).

SERVES 4-6

House Salad
WITH SUN-DRIED TOMATO DRESSING

▸ **SALAD**

1 head romaine lettuce,
torn into bite-size pieces

1 small cucumber, peeled and diced

1 large tomato, cut into chunks

1 carrot, thinly sliced

8-10 small pitted green olives

Small cubes of Swiss or
cheddar cheese (optional)

▸ **SUN-DRIED TOMATO DRESSING**
(Yield: 2 cups)

1 clove garlic, peeled

1/2 small onion

2 tablespoons oil-packed sun-dried tomatoes, drained

2 tablespoons grated Parmesan cheese

1 tablespoon granulated sugar

1/2 teaspoon salt

1/8 teaspoon freshly ground black pepper

1 teaspoon dried oregano

1/2 cup red wine vinegar

1 cup canola oil

In a large bowl, combine lettuce, cucumber, tomato, carrot, olives and cheese (if using).
Toss with 1/2 to 1 cup of Sun-Dried Tomato Dressing.

In a blender container, place garlic, onion, tomatoes, cheese, sugar, salt, pepper,
oregano and vinegar. With blender running, add oil in a slow, steady stream.

SERVES 4-6

Pasta
PIZZA

- 1 tablespoon light olive oil

  8 ounces angel hair pasta, cooked
  and drained (do not rinse)

  2 6-ounce cans tomato paste

  1 3 1/2-ounce package pepperoni slices

  8 ounces shredded mozzarella cheese

  1/2 cup grated Parmesan cheese

  1 teaspoon dried oregano

Preheat oven to 400°. Oil the bottom of a 12" ovenproof skillet or pizza pan. Place pasta in pan and spread evenly over pan. Spread tomato paste over pasta. Place pepperoni slices on tomato paste to cover. Sprinkle with mozzarella and Parmesan. Sprinkle oregano over all. Cook on top of stove over medium heat for 3-5 minutes to form a light crust. Place in oven 10-15 minutes. Cut with pizza wheel and serve at once.

NOTE: Toppings of your choice may be added: olives, mushrooms, sausage, etc.

SERVES 4

Antipasto PLATTER

On a large platter of assorted lettuces and/or field greens, arrange any or all of the following:

- Rolled anchovies
  Baby corn
  Black olives
  Green olives
  Cherry tomatoes
  Pickled okra
  Pepperoni slices
  Cubes of Jarlsberg or other cheeses
  Deviled egg halves
  Gherkins
  Garbanzos
  Halves of cooked small new potatoes topped with sour cream and red caviar

SERVES 6-8

Quick Ways to
DESSERT

Quick Ways
TO DESSERT

PAN-BAKED APPLES
with Orange Custard Sauce

▶ 1 cup plus 3 tablespoons granulated sugar, divided

2 cups water

4 apples, peeled, cut in half and seeded

3 egg yolks

1 cup heavy cream, scalded

2 tablespoons orange liqueur

Raisins and chopped pecans for garnish

APPLES: In a large skillet, bring 1 cup sugar and the water to a boil over medium heat. Allow mixture to cook 2-3 minutes or until sugar has dissolved. Add apple halves to pan, cut side down; cover and cook until apples begin to soften, about 15 minutes. Remove apples and cooking liquid to a bowl. Cool, then refrigerate.

SAUCE: In the top of a double boiler, place egg yolks and remaining 3 tablespoons sugar over gently boiling water. Whisk together to mix well. Add scalded cream and stir constantly until mixture begins to thicken. Strain mixture into a bowl. When cool, stir in liqueur and refrigerate.

TO SERVE: Place 2 apple halves in each of 4 dessert dishes or bowls. Drizzle with the sauce and sprinkle with raisins and nuts.

SERVES 4

Banana
SMOOTHIE

- 1 pint fat-free vanilla yogurt
- 1 banana, peeled and sliced

Place yogurt and banana into work bowl of food processor fitted with steel blade. Blend until well combined. Pour into dessert glasses (martini glasses work well) and serve at once.

SERVES 4

BANANAS
Flambé

- ▸ 2 tablespoons brown sugar
  1 tablespoon butter
  1 ripe banana, peeled and sliced lengthwise
  Dash of ground cinnamon
  1 tablespoon brandy
  2 tablespoons rum

In a chafing dish or skillet, melt the sugar with the butter. Add the banana and sauté until tender but not soft, 3-4 minutes. Sprinkle with cinnamon. Spoon brandy and rum over the bananas and ignite. Baste with warm liquid until flame burns out. Serve at once over ice cream or topped with whipped cream and a cherry.

SERVES 2

BANANA SPLIT
Sundae

- 1 scoop vanilla ice cream (or flavor of choice)

  1/2 banana, sliced

  1 tablespoon chopped pecans or walnuts (or both)

  3 or 4 maraschino cherries

  2 tablespoons fresh blueberries

  Drizzles of chocolate, strawberry and caramel sauce

Place ice cream in a dessert bowl. Top with banana slices, nuts, cherries and blueberries. Drizzle with sauces and serve.

SERVES 1
(Or share with someone you love!)

Orange
FLOAT

▶ 1 large scoop vanilla ice cream
1 12-ounce can of orange soda, chilled

Place ice cream in a large, chilled glass.
Pour cold orange soda over ice cream.
Serve with a straw and a spoon.

SERVES 1

TRIPLE
Orange Delight

- 1/4 cup sweet orange marmalade
  2 tablespoons orange juice
  2 teaspoons orange liqueur
  1 scoop orange sherbet or orange/vanilla swirl ice cream
  Orange slices for garnish
  Mint leaves for garnish

In a small saucepan over low heat, combine the marmalade and orange juice. Heat and stir just until well mixed. Cool. Add the liqueur and continue to cool to room temperature.

To serve, place sherbet it a dessert glass or bowl.
Spoon 2 tablespoons orange sauce over.
Garnish with orange slices and mint leaves.

SERVES 1

Peaches
IN PORT

▸ 6 peaches
  1/2 cup granulated sugar
  1 cup port wine
  1 cup blueberries, divided
  Whipped cream for garnish

Peel peaches and cut into large chunks. Place in large saucepan and cover with sugar. Add port and cook over medium-low heat until tender, about 5 minutes. Remove peaches and liquid to a bowl. Cool, then refigerate until cold, 2-3 hours or overnight.

When cold, remove peaches from refrigerator and drain; reserve 1/4 cup liquid. Place 1/2 cup blueberries and reserved liquid from peaches in a medium bowl. Lightly crush berries with a fork. Toss remaining whole berries with drained peaches. Spoon crushed blueberry liquid over mixture. Ladle into serving bowls, garnish with whipped cream and serve.

SERVES 4-6

RED, WHITE & BLUEBERRY Parfaits

▸ 2 cups heavy cream

2 tablespoons confectioners' sugar

2 cups raspberries

2 cups blueberries

In a large mixing bowl, whip the cream with the sugar until stiff peaks form. In 4 champagne flutes, layer the ingredients 1 to 1 1/2" deep in this order: blueberries, whipped cream, raspberries, whipped cream. Top with a raspberry and 2 or 3 blueberries.

SERVES 4

RASPBERRY
Rendezvous

- 1 12-ounce jar red raspberry preserves
- 1 10-ounce package frozen raspberries, thawed
- 2 tablespoons raspberry liqueur

- 1 scoop raspberry sorbet
- 3-4 slices kiwi for garnish
- 5-6 blackberries for garnish

Place raspberry preserves and raspberries in work bowl of a food processor and process until well combined. Strain mixture into a bowl. Add liqueur and mix well. Refrigerate until ready to serve.

Place sorbet in a stemmed glass. Garnish with kiwi and blackberries. Drizzle with raspberry sauce.

SERVES 1

Chocolate-Dipped
FRUIT CHUNKS

▸ 1/4 cup (1/2 stick) butter

8 ounces semisweet chocolate

1 cup brown sugar

1/2 cup brewed coffee

1 1/2 teaspoons instant coffee granules

2 tablespoons coffee liqueur

1/2 cup heavy cream

2 cups strawberries

2 cups seedless grapes

1 pineapple, cut into chunks

1 cantaloupe and/or honeydew, seeded and cut into chunks

Mint leaves for garnish

In a medium saucepan over low heat, melt butter. Add chocolate, sugar, brewed coffee, coffee granules, liqueur and cream. Stir constantly until chocolate has melted and ingredients are well combined. Cool to room temperature.

For individual servings, place a small ramekin filled with chocolate sauce in the center of a dessert bowl. Surround ramekin with chunks of assorted fruit. Garnish with mint leaves.

SERVES 6-8

CHOCOLATE
Pots de Crème

▸ 1 cup semisweet chocolate chips

1 1/4 cups light cream, scalded

2 egg yolks

2 tablespoons brandy

Whipped cream (optional)

Place the chocolate chips, hot cream, egg yolks and brandy into a blender or food processor and process on high speed until smooth. Pour into 4 ramekins or dessert glasses. Chill until set, about 3 hours or overnight. Top with whipped cream, if desired.

SERVES 4

GOOEY
Brownies

- 2 squares (1 ounce) unsweetened chocolate
- 1 stick (4 ounces) butter
- 2 eggs
- 1 cup sugar
- 1 teaspoon vanilla
- 1/2 cup flour

- 1/8 teaspoon salt
- 1/2 cup pecans, chopped
- 1/2 cup macadamia nuts, chopped
- 1/4 cup dark chocolate chunks
- 1/4 cup white chocolate chips

Preheat oven to 350°.

Melt chocolate and butter. Remove from heat. In mixer bowl, beat eggs until thick. Gradually add sugar and beat until mixture is thick and fluffy. Stir in vanilla and melted chocolate-butter mixture. Blend in flour and salt. Fold in nuts and chocolate chunks and chips. Bake in a greased 8" square pan until shiny crust forms, about 22-25 minutes. Cool. Loosen around edges with a sharp knife and cut into squares.

NOTE: Brownies will appear to be underbaked. When cooled, they will set and be gooey.

YIELD: 16-20 brownies

COOKIE
Hash

- 1 cup heavy cream
  1 tablespoon granulated sugar
  1 tablespoon orange liqueur
  1/4 cup blueberries
  1/4 cup blackberries
  1/4 cup raspberries
  1/4 cup quartered strawberries
  6 graham crackers, crumbled into small bite size pieces
  6 cream-filled chocolate cookies, crumbled into small bite-size pieces

Place cream in a mixing bowl. Add sugar and liqueur and whip until soft peaks form. Add blueberries, blackberries, raspberries, strawberries, graham cracker pieces and chocolate cookie pieces. Mix just to combine ingredients. Refrigerate 1-2 hours. Serve in small stemmed wine glasses. Top with a chocolate cookie or sliced strawberry, if desired.

SERVES 4

EVERYTHING
Cookies

- 6 tablespoons butter, softened

  1/2 cup light brown sugar

  1/4 cup granulated sugar

  1 teaspoon vanilla extract

  1 egg

  1 1/2 cups all-purpose flour

  1/2 teaspoon baking soda

  1/4 teaspoon salt

  1/2 cup chopped pecans

  1/4 cup sliced almonds

  1/4 cup coarsley chopped macadamia nuts

  1 10-ounce package semisweet chocolate chunks

  1/2 cup white chocolate chips

Preheat oven to 350°.

In a large mixer bowl, cream the butter, brown sugar, granulated sugar and vanilla until light and fluffy. Add egg and beat well. In another bowl, combine the flour, baking soda and salt; add to butter-egg mixture. Stir in nuts and chocolate chunks. Drop by tablespoonfuls onto parchment-lined cookie sheets. Bake 10-12 minutes or until lightly browned. Cool. Remove from cookie sheets to wire rack.

YIELD: 2-3 dozen cookies

Mocha
TORTONI

▸ 2 cups miniature marshmallows
1 1/2 tablespoons instant coffee granules
1/2 cup boiling water
1/4 cup chopped pecans
1/4 cup semisweet mini chocolate chips
1 cup heavy cream, whipped

Place marshmallows and coffee in a bowl.
Add water and stir until marshmallows dissolve.
Refrigerate, stirring occasionally, until thick and
syrupy. Add pecans and chocolate chips; fold in
whipped cream. Freeze either in individual serving
dishes or a 1 1/2 quart freezer-proof dish.

SERVES 6-8

NOTES

INDEX

About the
AUTHOR

Doris Koplin has cooked since she was eight years old.
Urged to enter baking contests by her high school home
economics teacher, and further inspired by the reward
of blue ribbons that followed, she was hooked on food.

Trained at a European cooking school, she has studied and
worked with many of the country's finest culinary teachers
and chefs. In her multi-faceted career, she has served as
cooking teacher, cooking school director, corporate chef,
product developer, recipe and menu designer and consultant
to chefs, caterers, restaurants and farmers' markets.

Doris is passionate and enthusiastic about her work.
She believes that dinner should be abundantly beautiful,
sensuous, and above all, taste divine.

She is pleased to present *The Quick Cook*, a delicious
collection of ideas for family dinners.